ABSOLUTE BEGINNERS

Guitar Scales

HAL•LEONARD®

Exclusive Distributors:
Hal Leonard
7777 West Bluemound Road,
Milwaukee, WI 53213
Email: info@halleonard.com
Hal Leonard Europe Limited
42 Wigmore Street Maryleborne,
London, WIU 2 RN
Email: info@halleonardeurope.com
Hal Leonard Australia Pty. Ltd.
4 Lentara Court Cheltenham,
Victoria, 9132 Australia
Email: info@halleonard.com.au

Order No. AM969672
ISBN 0-7119-8772-6
This book © Copyright 2003 by Hal Leonard

Written by Cliff Douse.
Editing and book layout by Sorcha Armstrong.
Music processing by Simon Troup and Paul Ewers.
Cover and text photographs by George Taylor.
Artist photographs courtesy of London Features International. Cover design
by Chloë Alexander.
Models: Jim Benham and Helen Sanderson.
CD produced by Cliff Douse.
CD mastered by Jonas Persson.

Printed in EU.

www.halleonard.com

Contents

Introduction 4

Tuning up 5

The fingerboard 6

Hand and finger positions 7

Guitar tablature 8

Special techniques 9

What are scales? 10

E minor pentatonic 11

The blues scale 12

Transposing scales 13

F minor pentatonic 14

G minor pentatonic 15

Your first 12-bar blues 16

Using the whole neck 17

A minor pentatonic 18

Playing lead guitar 20

Easy blues licks 21

Blues solo 22

Country blues 24

The major scale 25

The natural minor scale 29

The modes 33

Advice on soloing 38

Classic guitar solos 39

CD track list 40

Introduction

Welcome to Absolute Beginners Guitar Scales. Scales are an essential tool for all guitar players; they allow you to play melodies and improvise solos over chord progressions. Every guitarist who has ever played lead lines, from Jimi Hendrix to Hank Marvin, and from Brian May to Noel Gallagher, has used scales to play them.

Our easy-to-follow instructions will guide you through:

- how to tune your guitar
- knowing the fingerboard
- understanding scales
- learning your first scales
- playing riffs and a solo
- playing a famous tune

You will find recordings of all the examples in this book on the accompanying CD, along with backing tracks for you to play along with.

Practise scales regularly; fifteen minutes every day is much better than a couple of hours once a week.

Whether you play acoustic or electric guitar, this book will help you to become a better all-round guitar player. Have fun!

You won't be able to play scales properly unless your guitar is in tune. There are various ways of tuning the guitar – choose the one that suits you best.

1. Use our CD

Track 1 of the CD gives tuning notes for each string, beginning with the 6th (lowest).

2. Relative tuning

Let's assume the bottom string (6th) is in tune. Being the thickest, you'll find that the 6th string probably won't drift out of tune as much as some of the others.

Now play the 5th fret note on the 6th string – and then play the open A string. They should sound the same. If not, adjust the tuning peg until they do. Repeat this step for all strings, except the G string (3rd string). See the diagrams below:

3. Use an electronic tuner

These are fairly cheap devices that you can buy from any guitar shop.

4. Tune to another instrument

The simplest way to make sure that your guitar is in tune is to find someone else with a tuned guitar and match each string on your guitar with the relevant string on the tuned guitar. Alternatively, you could tune to a piano or electronic keyboard.

Tip

If you're playing with other people it's vital that you all tune to the same note. If one of the instruments can't be easily tuned (like a piano for example), make sure that you tune to that.

Relative Tuning Guide

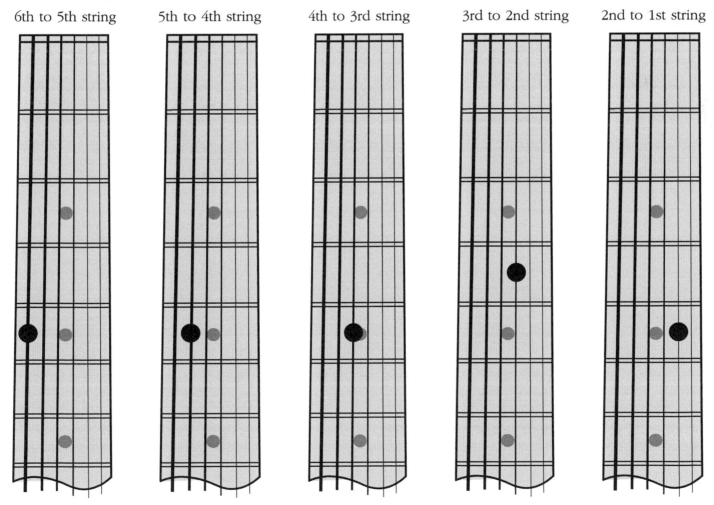

6th to 5th string   5th to 4th string   4th to 3rd string   3rd to 2nd string   2nd to 1st string

The fingerboard

Every scale begins and ends on a 'root' note and this note gives the scale its letter name. If you know all of the note names on the bottom E string (the thickest string) you can determine where to start your scale.

For example, you can play a C major scale by using a major scale shape, and starting at C on the 8th fret, or a D major scale by starting at the 10th fret. There are 12 keys in all, so every time you learn one new scale shape, you can play 12 new scales!

Some of the notes below have symbols next to their letters. A sharp (♯) symbol *raises* the pitch of the note by one semitone (which is one fret on your guitar). A flat symbol (♭) *lowers* the pitch in the same way.

You will also notice that every sharp has an equivalent flat (for instance C♯ is the same as D♭). It is important to remember this as you will come across some scales and songs that have sharp notes while others have flats.

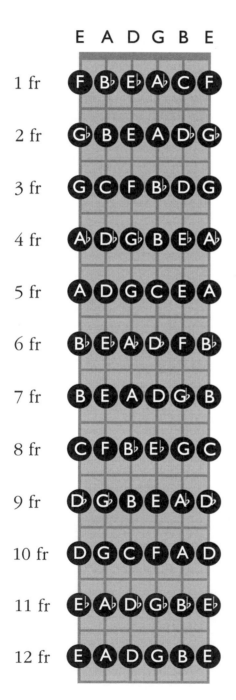

Use this diagram if you want to find the root note of a scale with a *flat* in its name.

Use this diagram if you want to find the root note of a scale with a *sharp* in its name.

If your hand and finger posture is good, you will be able to play scales more cleanly, fluidly and rapidly. Here are some notes of guidance to make sure that your picking and fretting techniques will help rather than hinder you.

Right Hand

Rest your right forearm lightly on the guitar's body and position your hand within easy contact of the strings. If you're using a pick, hold it between your thumb and index finger as shown below. To play simple melodies, strike the appropriate strings with a downstroke for each note and, for faster passages, alternate between upstrokes and downstrokes. Alternatively, you may use your thumb and fingers to pluck strings in a classical style (shown right).

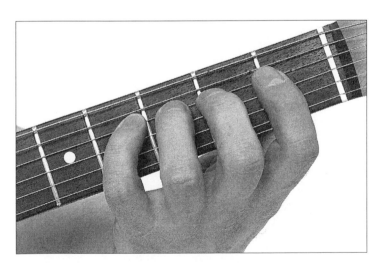

Left Hand

The fingers on your left hand press down the fretboard in order to sound out the notes. It is important to press down just behind a fret to produce a clean, ringing tone. If you put your finger on top of the fret you will muffle the string and if you place it too far back, it will make the string rattle against the fret to give a nasty buzzing sound.

All scale shapes in this book are based on the 'one-finger-per-fret' system – each finger has a fret space to itself – pictured on the left. In each of the scale shapes in this book, every note has a circle with a number in it. The numbers tell you which finger you should use to play the note:

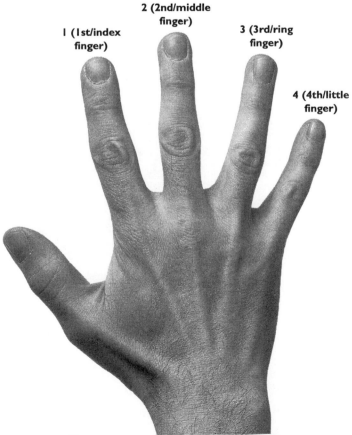

Tip

If you're left-handed, you will be fretting the scale notes with your right hand and picking them with your left.

Guitar tablature

Tablature (TAB) is the easiest way to learn tunes on the guitar. It features six horizontal lines under a conventional music stave, each representing a guitar string. The numbers on these lines tell you which frets should be played.

The Music Stave shows pitches and rhythms and is divided by lines into bars. Pitches are named after the first seven letters of the alphabet.

Tablature graphically represents the guitar fingerboard. Each horizontal line represents a string, and each number represents a fret.

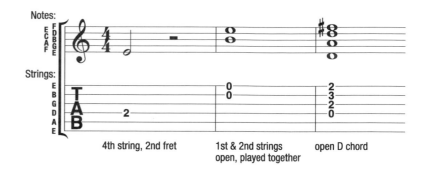

4th string, 2nd fret   1st & 2nd strings open, played together   open D chord

Hammer-on

This is when you play a note on a string and then hammer down with another left-hand finger to produce another note on the same string. The example here is telling you to play the note at the 12th fret on the 3rd string and then hammer down on the 14th fret to produce the next note.

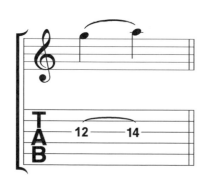

Pull-off

This is the opposite of a hammer-on. In this example, you are asked to play the note at the 14th fret on the 4th string and then pull your finger off, slightly plucking the string, and allowing the note at the 12th fret to ring out. You have to be holding down the note at the 14th fret in advance for this to work.

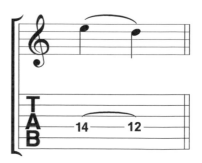

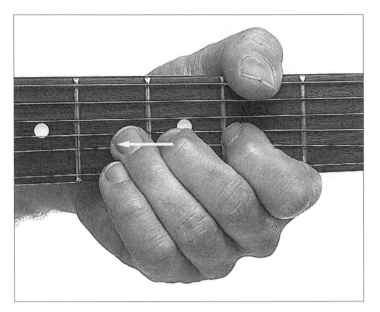

Slide

You can perform a slide simply by playing a note and then moving the finger that is holding down that note to another position on the same string. You must keep your finger held down on the neck for this to work. You can slide up or down the fingerboard.

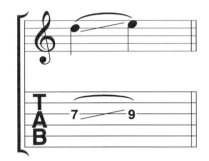

Bend

You can 'bend' a note by up to a tone and a half by pushing it up the fingerboard while you are holding it down. Here, we are bending a note at the 12th fret on the 3rd string so that it sounds like the note at the 14th fret.

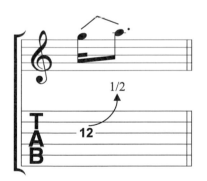

Vibrato

Bend a note up very slightly, then release the bend, and repeat over and over. If you do this very rapidly, you'll create vibrato.

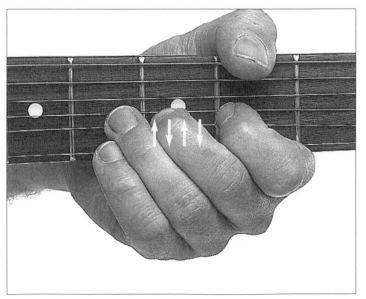

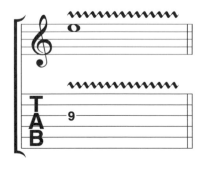

What are scales?

Scales are groups of notes played in ascending or descending order of pitch. These can be used to create melodies and solo improvisations.

There are many different scales and each one has its own name and distinct character. The major scale has a pleasant, melodic sound that you will recognise from many types of upbeat music, while the natural minor scale has a melancholy character that makes it ideal for ballads; the blues scale has a very distinctive sound that reminds you of the type of music it got its name from; and the phrygian mode, a more exotic kind of scale, has a very Spanish feel.

Intervals

Each of the notes in the scales listed in this book are separated by intervals. The smallest interval between two notes is called a semitone (S) and two semitones make a tone (T). Frets are separated by one semitone.

E string

In this example, A and B♭ are one semitone (fret) apart. Play the notes at the 5th and 6th frets on the bottom E string, and listen to how they sound.

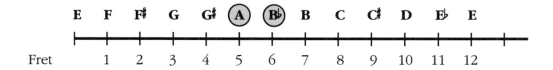

Now the notes are a tone apart – A and B. Play them and listen to the difference between a semitone and a tone.

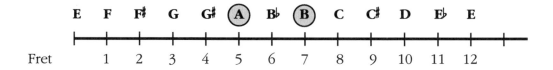

Some scales, such as the pentatonic scales, even have some notes that are a tone and a half (a tone plus a semitone) apart, like this:

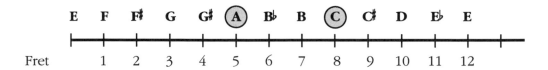

Fact

The technical name for an interval of three semitones is a 'tritone' and in olden times, was thought to be the 'devil's' interval (due to its discordant sound)!

The easiest scales to learn are ones played in the 'open position'. These scales combine open string notes with fretted ones.

Here is the E minor pentatonic scale, a scale that has been used by countless blues, rock and pop guitar players.

Start at the bottom open E string and work upwards, following the tab and diagram. The diagram shows the guitar neck with the nut at the left and the 6th (thickest) string at the bottom. The numbers indicate which finger to use to play the note. Numbers in black circles indicate the root notes of the scale – useful for when you want to transpose them.

Em pentatonic

Listen to the CD for a demonstration of how this should sound.

Track 2 demonstration

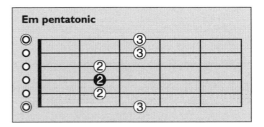

Em pentatonic

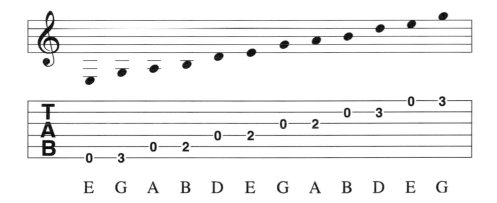

E   G   A   B   D   E   G   A   B   D   E   G

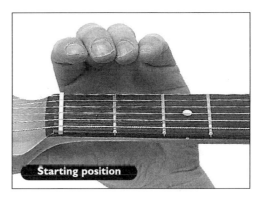

Starting position

Congratulations – you've just played your first scale! Easy, wasn't it? Now play the same scale the other way around, from the highest note to the lowest:

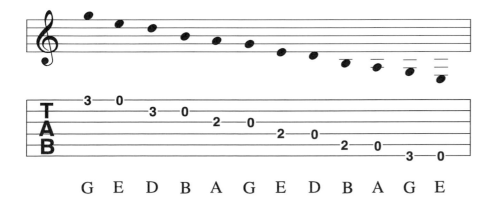

G   E   D   B   A   G   E   D   B   A   G   E

To simplify, the rest of the scales in this book will be shown only in their ascending form, although you will hear ascending and descending forms on the CD.

Practise with a metronome if you want to improve your timing.

The blues scale

Add another note between the 3rd and 4th notes of the pentatonic minor scale and you will have the blues scale, a scale that has often been used by John Lee Hooker and other legendary blues and rock guitar players.

E blues scale

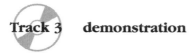 Track 3   demonstration

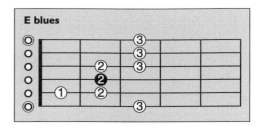

E blues

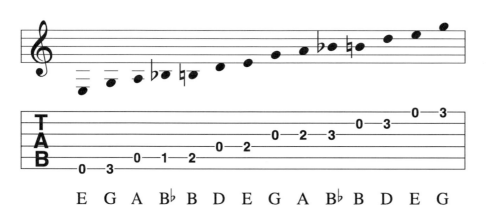

E   G   A   B♭   B   D   E   G   A   B♭   B   D   E   G

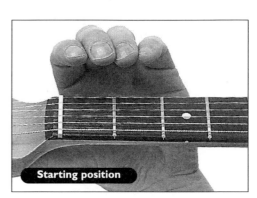

Starting position

Mini Blues riff in E

Here's a really easy blues riff for you to try using the E blues scale. It only consists of four notes. Listen to the CD and then try to play along.

Track 4   demonstration   Track 5   backing track

This symbol is called a **repeat sign** and indicates that you should go back to the beginning and play through again.

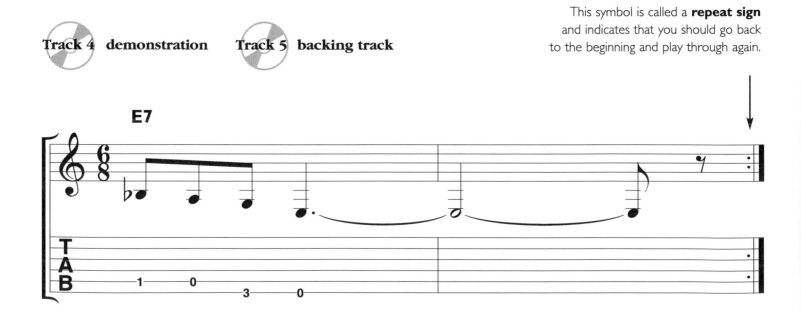

Transposing scales on a guitar is extremely easy. Because of the way the notes are laid out on the guitar fingerboard, the fingering 'shape' of a scale is always the same, no matter what key it is played in.

Once you have learned that shape, all you have to do to change the scale's key is move its shape to a different position on the fretboard. Here's how you do it...

Em pentatonic

Let's look at the E minor pentatonic scale. This scale starts on the note produced by the open 6th string (E). Because of this, we have put a circle around the open E in the diagram.

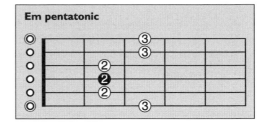

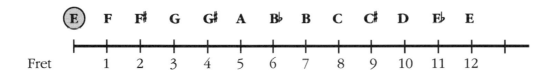

Fm pentatonic

If, however, you want to play the same scale in the key of F instead, simply move the whole scale shape up one fret so that you are starting on F instead:

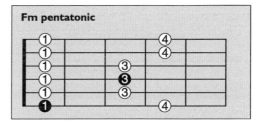

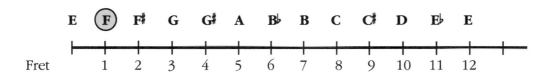

Gm pentatonic

And if you want to play it in the key of G, move the shape up to the third fret so it starts on G – it's as easy as that! Refer to the fretboard diagrams on page 6 to check note names and fret positions.

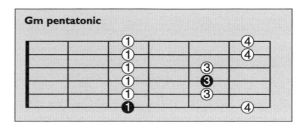

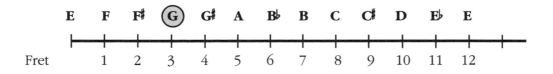

F minor pentatonic

This principle works for all of the other keys. Let's try it in practice with a few pentatonic scales on the guitar. Here's the E minor pentatonic scale again with its fingering shape:

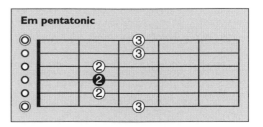

Em pentatonic

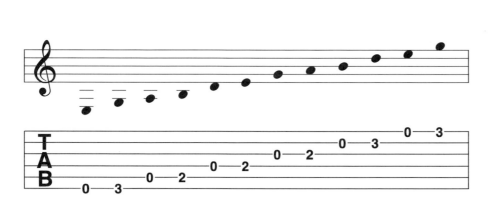

E G A B D E G A B D E G

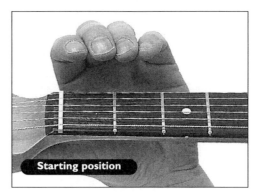

Starting position

Fm pentatonic

If you want to play the same scale in F, all you have to do is move the whole scale shape up a fret like this:

Track 6 demonstration

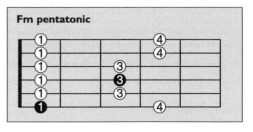

Fm pentatonic

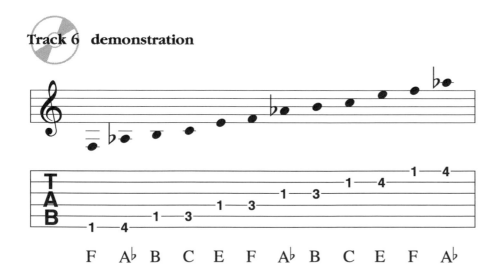

F Ab B C E F Ab B C E F Ab

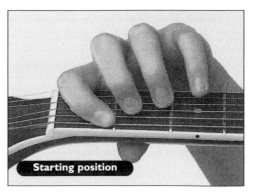

Starting position

If you play the same shape starting from the 3rd fret (the note G) you are now playing in the key of G.

In the fretbox, you'll notice that there's a number underneath the dots (3fr) – this denotes that the shape you are looking at should start at the third fret. This is a very common abbreviation, especially in guitar chord boxes.

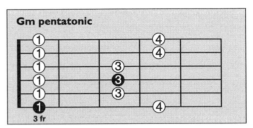

Challenge

Can you transpose the minor pentatonic scale into the following keys: Cm and Am? Look at the diagram on page 6 to work out what fret to start on.

Track 7   **demonstration**

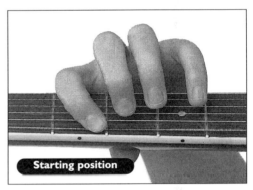

Gm pentatonic

Starting position

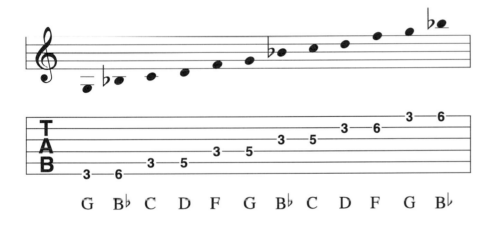

G B♭ C D F G B♭ C D F G B♭

HINTS & TIPS

• Learn all of the notes on the guitar's 6th string and you'll be able to transpose any scale shape you know into any key you want. This makes the process of learning scales much quicker.

• Try playing the pentatonic minor and blues scales in all of the twelve different keys; you'll be surprised at how quickly you know each and every one of them!

• Always practise scales in both their ascending (up) and descending (down) forms.

Your first 12-bar blues

The following blues sequence starts with the blues scale in E in the open position, moves up to the A blues scale at the 5th fret and then goes back to the E blues scale at the open position.

It then switches to the B pentatonic minor scale at the 7th fret, the A pentatonic minor at the 5th fret and returns to the E blues scale in the open position. Don't worry – it's not as complicated as it sounds!

12-bar blues riff in E

Track 8 demonstration   Track 9 backing track

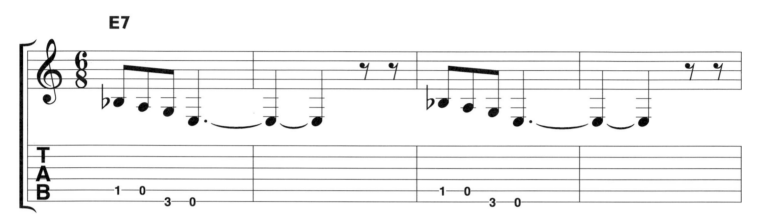

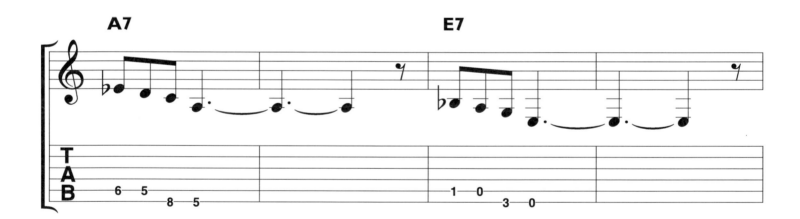

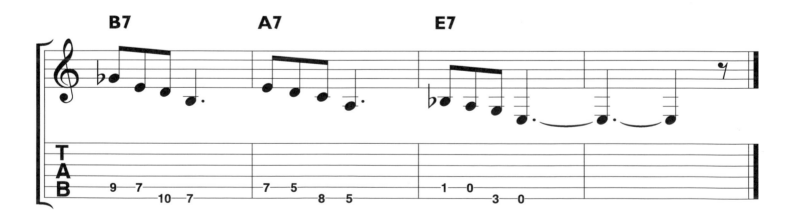

Now play the backing track and try it by yourself.

To really extend your capabilities, you'll need to learn some different shapes for the same scale, so you won't be stuck playing that same old pentatonic lick every time you break into a solo! So let's look at all of the pentatonic minor scale shapes in the key of A.

Shape 1 is the first of five shapes that can be used to play the A minor pentatonic scale all over the guitar fingerboard. Because this shape starts on the root note of the scale (in this case 'A'), it is the most important shape and the easiest one to find on the guitar.

Am pentatonic Shape 1

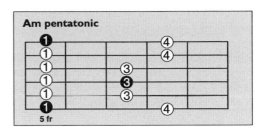

Track 10 demonstration

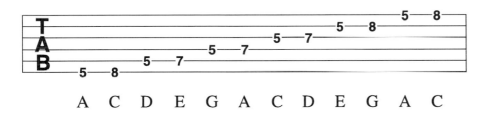

A C D E G A C D E G A C

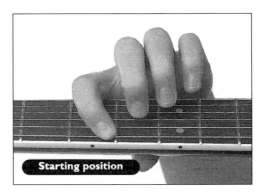

Starting position

The other four pentatonic shapes do not start on the root note, but their different patterns encourage players to do different things with the scale.

They also unlock the key to the whole fingerboard – if you know how to play a scale over the whole fingerboard, you are freer to express yourself with it.

CHECKPOINT

WHAT YOU'VE ACHIEVED SO FAR...

You can now:
- Hold your guitar comfortably and tune it
- Read and understand guitar tablature
- Play the minor pentatonic and blues scales
- Recognise note names
- Play a 12-bar blues!

A minor pentatonic

Am pentatonic Shape 2

Shape 2 of the A minor pentatonic scale starts with the note C on the 8th fret. Start this scale with the 2nd finger of your fretting hand.

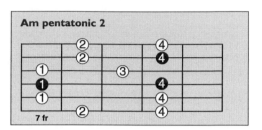

Am pentatonic 2

Track 11 demonstration

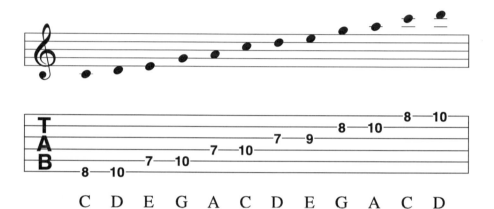

C D E G A C D E G A C D

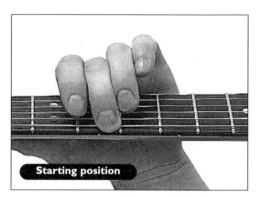

Starting position

Am pentatonic Shape 3

The next shape starts with 'D' played by the 2nd finger on the 10th fret. After the third string, you will have to adjust your hand position up one fret to play the notes on the top two strings.

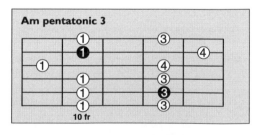

Am pentatonic 3

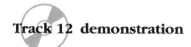

Track 12 demonstration

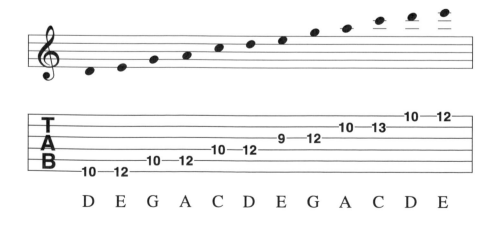

D E G A C D E G A C D E

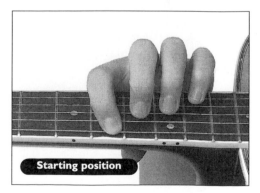

Starting position

Am pentatonic Shape 4

The fourth shape is easier to play because it again
starts with the first fretting finger:

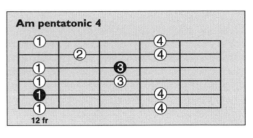

Am pentatonic 4

12 fr

Track 13 demonstration

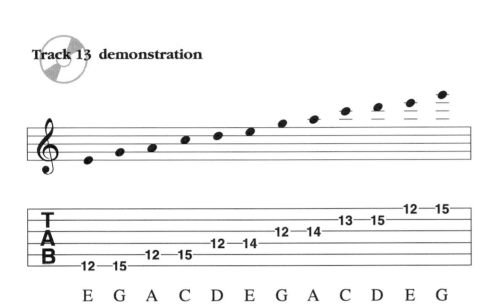

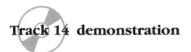

E G A C D E G A C D E G

Starting position

Am pentatonic Shape 5

And the fifth shape is one of the easiest to remember
because of its symmetry:

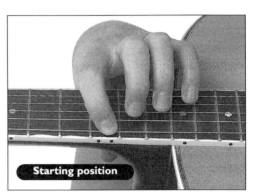

Am pentatonic 5

15 fr

Track 14 demonstration

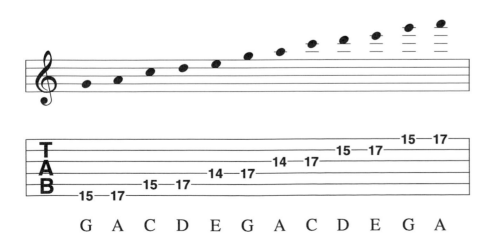

G A C D E G A C D E G A

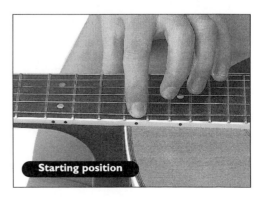

Starting position

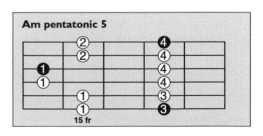

Playing lead guitar

Now that you've learnt all of the minor pentatonic shapes, you'll be wanting to play some music with them. Here are some techniques which you can use to put together a bluesy solo.

All of the examples use Shapes 1 and 2, but you should also work out how to play them in other positions on the fretboard.

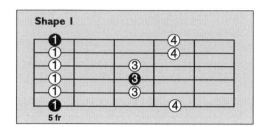

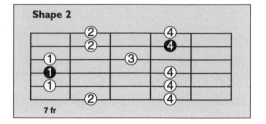

Slide

This is a slide. Play the note behind the 7th fret on the 3rd string with your 3rd finger and then slide that finger up to the 9th fret. You have to keep your finger pressed down for the slide to work.

 **Track 15** demonstration

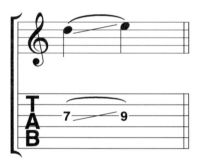

Half-tone Bend

Here, play the note behind the 7th fret on the 3rd string with your 3rd finger, but this time push the string upwards to reach a semitone higher (it will sound like the note at the 8th fret). You are now playing that extra note in the blues scale.

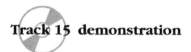 **Track 16** demonstration

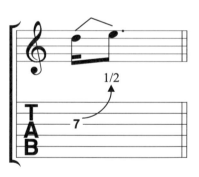

Bend & Release

When you reach the top of the bend, mute the 3rd string softly with your picking hand, bring it down to the original position and then play the note at the 7th fret again. Practise until you can do it smoothly and then try the blues licks on the next page.

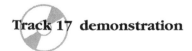 **Track 17** demonstration

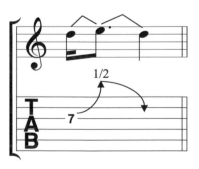

Track 18 Lick 1

Now that you're familiar with bends and slides, you can try your first easy lead guitar licks.

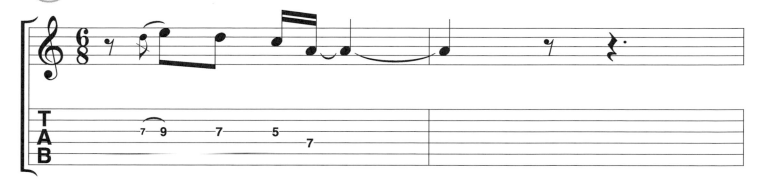

Track 19 Lick 2

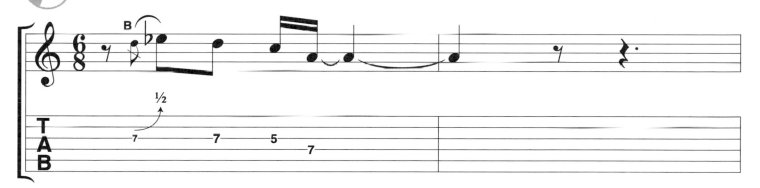

Track 20 Lick 3

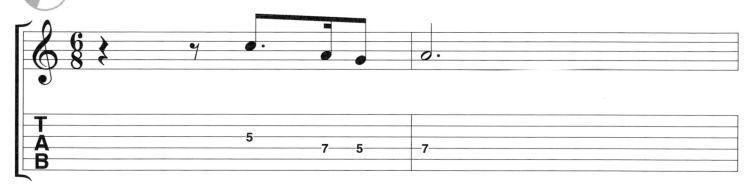

Track 21 Lick 4

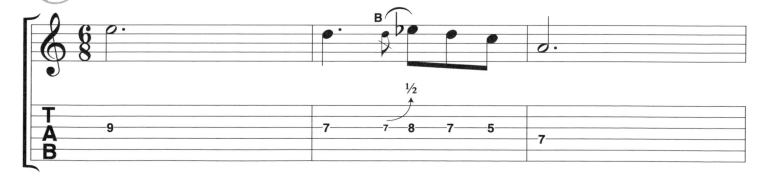

Blues solo

Now it's time to put all of these ideas into a solo.
The following example joins all of the riffs up with
a few extra notes:

12-bar blues solo in A

Track 22 demonstration   **Track 23 backing track**

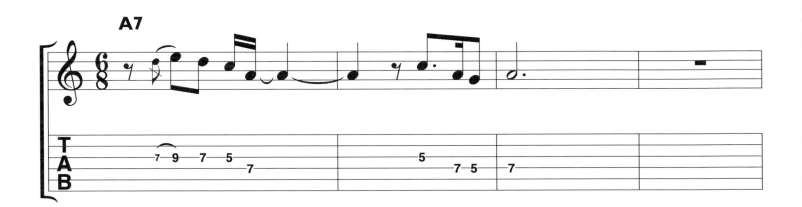

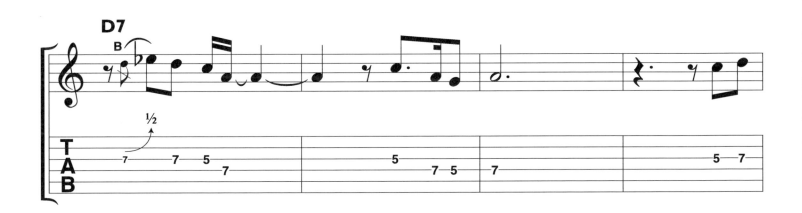

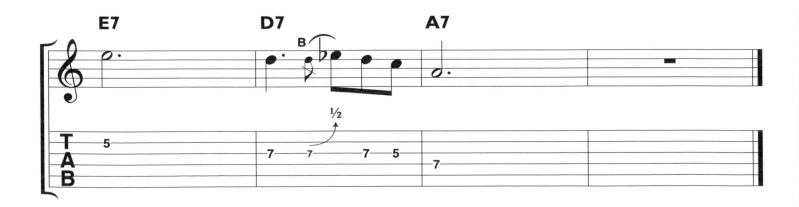

A maj Pentatonic

The major pentatonic is another commonly-used scale. In contrast to the moody minor, the major pentatonic scale has a bright, upbeat feel. Here it is in A.

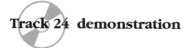

Track 24 demonstration

A   B   C♯   E   F♯   A   B   C♯   E   F♯   A

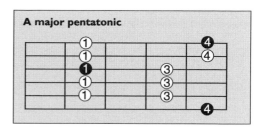

A major pentatonic

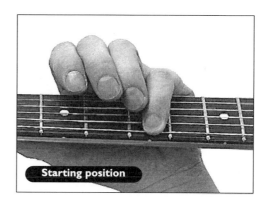

Starting position

A 'Country' Scale

The blues scale also has a variant known as the country scale, which basically makes more use of major scale tones than the blues scale. We've also shown it in A so you can compare the two scales.

Track 25 demonstration

A   B   C   C♯   E   F♯   A   B   C   C♯   E   F♯   A

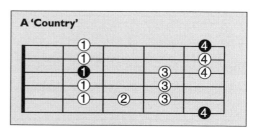

A 'Country'

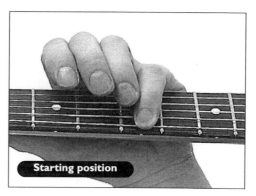

Starting position

Country blues

The major pentatonic and country scales also work over our 12-bar blues progression.

Why not try some other solo ideas over the backing track using the major pentatonic and country scales?

'Country' blues sequence

Track 26 demonstration   **Track 27 backing track**

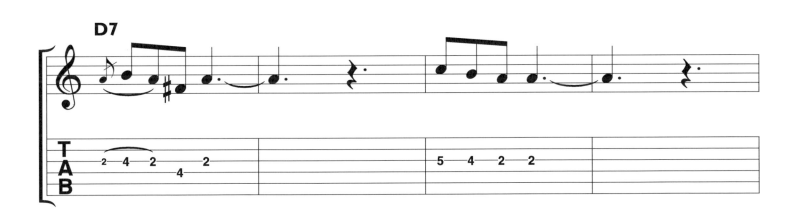

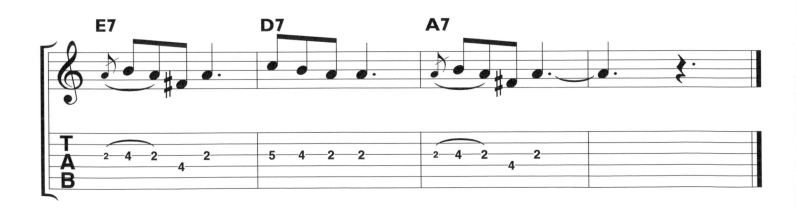

The major scale, with its instantly recognisable 'Do Re Mi' sound, is the most commonly used scale in music. It has been used to create more tunes than any other scale and it also provides the background for standard music theory as we know it.

There are five major scale shapes that cover the whole guitar neck and they are all worth learning, for if you are familiar with them, you will have a whole world of lead and melodic guitar at your fingertips.

G major Shape 1

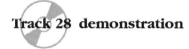

Track 28 demonstration

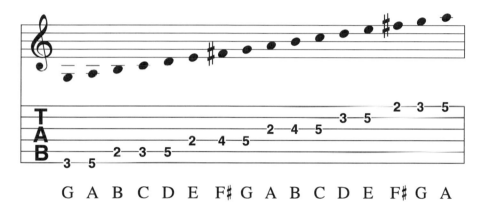

G A B C D E F♯ G A B C D E F♯ G A

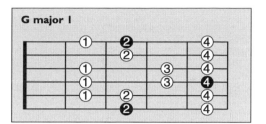

G major I

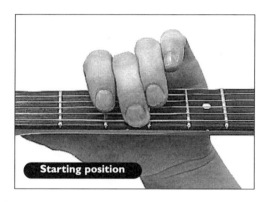

Starting position

The above shape is the most important major scale pattern as it begins on the tonic note and hence gives you an instant flavour of the scale. It is also easy to transpose into other keys in the way that we explained earlier in the book.

You will find that this scale finger pattern demands a bit more practice than the pentatonic scale shapes but if you stick to the 'one finger per fret' technique you'll get the hang of it in next to no time!

CHECKPOINT

WHAT YOU'VE ACHIEVED SO FAR...

You can now:
- Play five different minor pentatonic scale shapes
- Play and use the country scale
- Play lead guitar licks using hammer-ons and bends
- Play a blues solo

Major scale shapes

G major Shape 2

Shape 2 starts on the 5th fret (A) on the 6th string. You will have to move your overall hand position back one fret to comfortably play the notes behind the 4th fret on the 3rd and 4th strings:

Track 29 demonstration

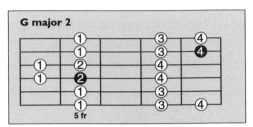

G major 2

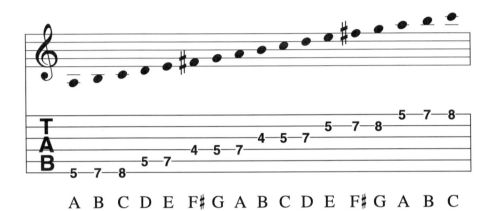

A B C D E F♯ G A B C D E F♯ G A B C

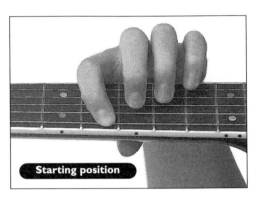

Starting position

G major Shape 3

And Shape 3 begins two frets further up the fingerboard:

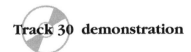

Track 30 demonstration

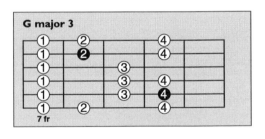

G major 3

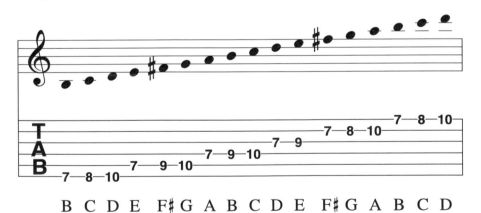

B C D E F♯ G A B C D E F♯ G A B C D

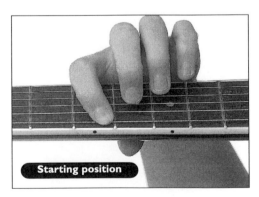

Starting position

G major Shape 4

Shape 4 begins with your 2nd finger behind the 10th fret on the 6th string:

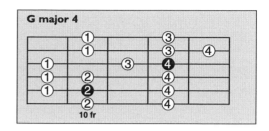

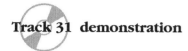
Track 31 demonstration

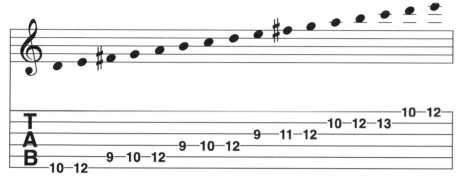

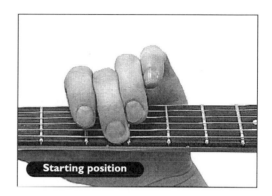
Starting position

D E F# G A B C D E F# G A B C D E

G major Shape 5

And Shape 5 begins on E, an octave higher than the open E string:

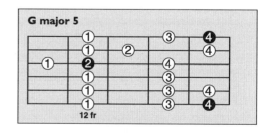

Track 32 demonstration

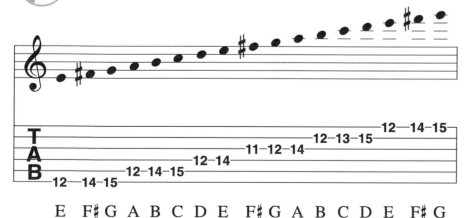

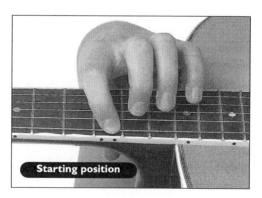
Starting position

E F# G A B C D E F# G A B C D E F# G

You can continue further up the neck by playing Shape 1 again at the 15th fret (an octave higher than in its original position), and so on.

Auld Lang Syne

This version uses Shape 1 of the G major scale. Why not try playing the tune using another one of the major scale shapes?

Track 33 demonstration   **Track 34** backing track

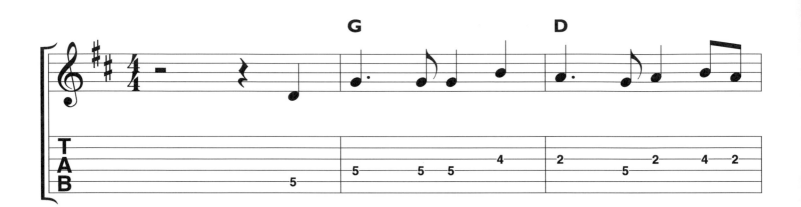

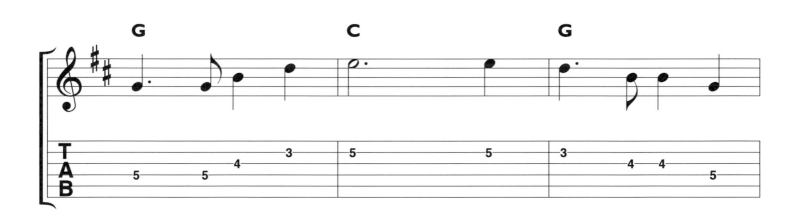

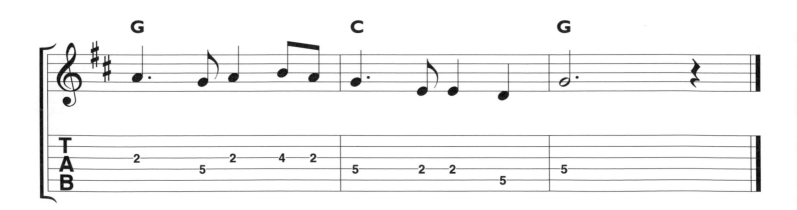

The natural minor scale, used for creating haunting melodies in ballads and scores, can be seen as a pentatonic minor scale with a couple of extra notes added. You'll see this when you look at the five natural minor guitar finger shapes.

You will also notice that all of the natural minor shapes are similar to the major scale ones we looked at in the previous section, but in different positions. There's a reason for that which will be explained later in the book.

G natural minor Shape 1

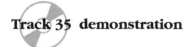 **Track 35 demonstration**

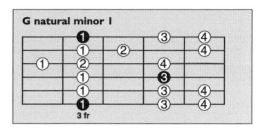

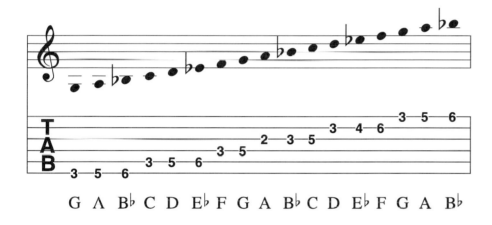

G A Bb C D Eb F G A Bb C D Eb F G A Bb

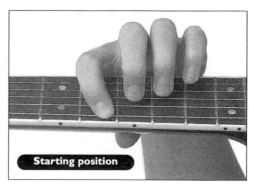

Starting position

G natural minor Shape 2

Track 36 demonstration

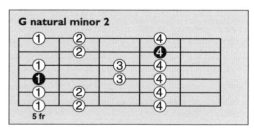

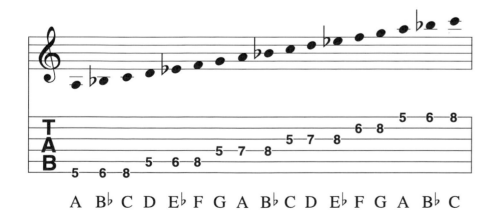

A Bb C D Eb F G A Bb C D Eb F G A Bb C

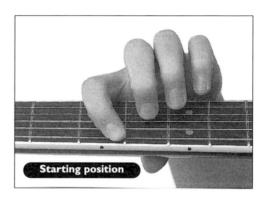

Starting position

Natural minor scale shapes

G natural minor Shape 3

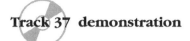

Track 37 demonstration

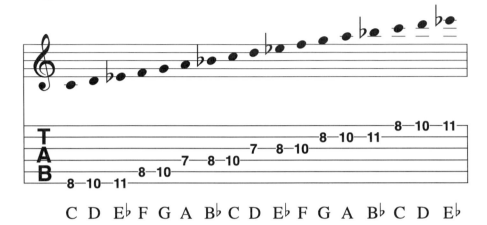

C D E♭ F G A B♭ C D E♭ F G A B♭ C D E♭

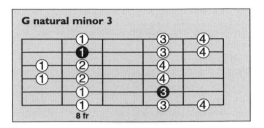

G natural minor 3

8 fr

Starting position

G natural minor Shape 4

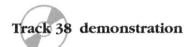

Track 38 demonstration

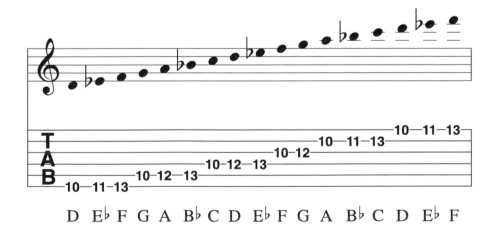

D E♭ F G A B♭ C D E♭ F G A B♭ C D E♭ F

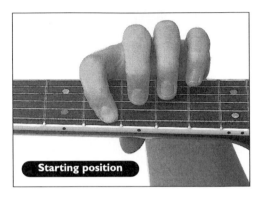

G natural minor 4

10 fr

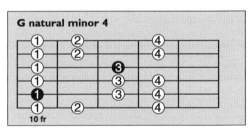

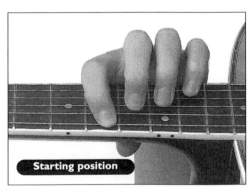

Starting position

G natural minor Shape 5

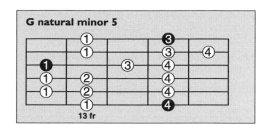

G natural minor 5

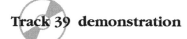
Track 39 demonstration

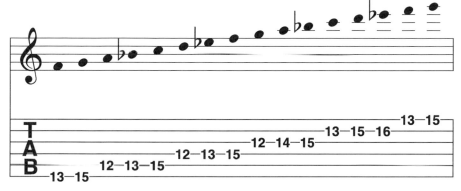

F G A B♭ C D E♭ F G A B♭ C D E♭ F G

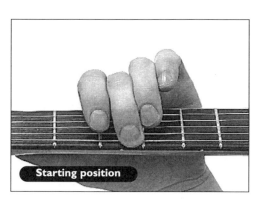

Starting position

Did you know?

Gary Moore, Mark Knopfler, Carlos Santana, Steve Hackett and Brian May are all well-known natural minor scale users.

Tips

• Learn all of the notes on the guitar's 6th string and you'll be able to transpose any scale shape you know into any key you want. This makes the process of learning scales much quicker.

• Try playing the pentatonic minor and blues scales in all of the twelve different keys; you'll be surprised at how quickly you know each and every one of them!

• Always practise scales in both their ascending (up) and descending (down) forms.

Natural minor in practice

Now use Shape 2 of the C natural minor scale to play this tune along with the backing track.

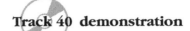 **Track 40 demonstration**

 **Track 41 backing track**

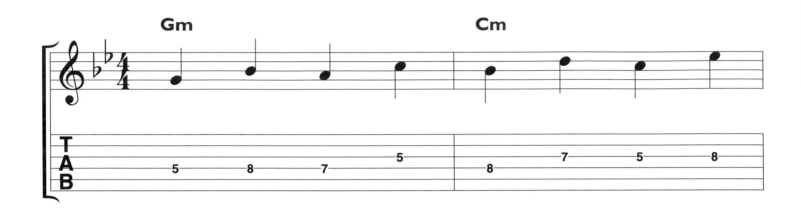

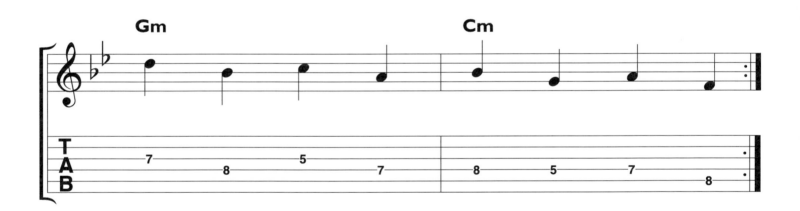

CHECKPOINT

WHAT YOU'VE ACHIEVED SO FAR...

You can now:
• Play five major scale shapes and use them in solos
• Play 'Auld Lang Syne'
• Use the natural minor scale in solos and riffs

You may have noticed that the natural minor scale shapes are similar to the major scale shapes, only they're played in different positions, and with different tonic notes. The reason for this is that they belong to the same scale family. The major scale family, as it's called, consists of seven modes. The first of these, the major scale itself, also known as the Ionian mode, has the formula 2212221 – where 1 is a semitone (one fret apart), and 2 is a tone (or two frets apart). The other modes are based on the other notes in that major scale. Even though all of the modes contain exactly the same notes, the different emphasis on tonic note gives each one a unique character. Here's the whole major scale modal family:

	I	2	3	4	5	6	7	8
Ionian	C _2_	D _2_	E _1_	F _2_	G _2_	A _2_	B _1_	C
Dorian	D _2_	E _1_	F _2_	G _2_	A _2_	B _1_	C _2_	D
Phrygrian	E _1_	F _2_	G _2_	A _2_	B _1_	C _2_	D _2_	E
Lydian	F _2_	G _2_	A _2_	B _1_	C _2_	D _2_	E _1_	F
Mixolydian	G _2_	A _2_	B _1_	C _2_	D _2_	E _1_	F _2_	G
Aeolian	A _2_	B _1_	C _2_	D _2_	E _1_	F _2_	G _2_	A
Locrian	B _1_	C _2_	D _2_	E _1_	F _2_	G _2_	A _2_	B

C Ionian

The Ionian mode is basically the major scale. It is shown here in C, for reference.

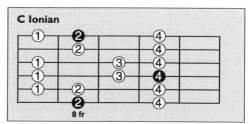

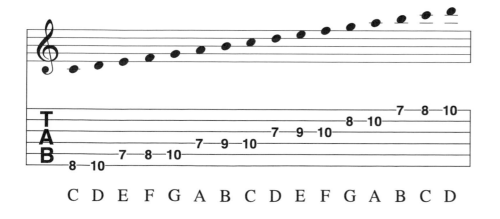

C D E F G A B C D E F G A B C D

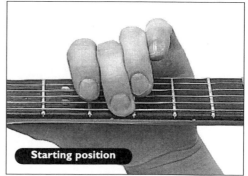

Starting position

The dorian mode

All of the modes in this section have been transposed into C for easy comparison. The ionian mode (major scale) and aeolian mode (natural minor scale) are not included here because they have already been covered earlier in the book in greater detail.

C Dorian

This is a minor sounding scale, which has been used by Dave Gilmour and Carlos Santana.

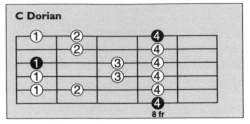

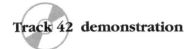 **Track 42** demonstration

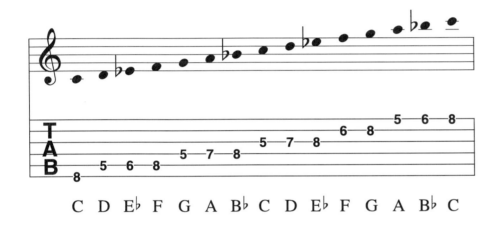

C D E♭ F G A B♭ C D E♭ F G A B♭ C

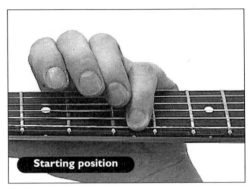

Starting position

Dorian groove

This riff is distinctly dorian! Play it along with the backing track on Track 44.

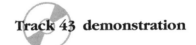 **Track 43** demonstration    **Track 44** backing track

C Phrygian

The Phrygian mode has a Spanish feel and is often used by Yngwie Mälmsteen and Paco de Lucia.

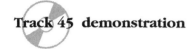 **Track 45 demonstration**

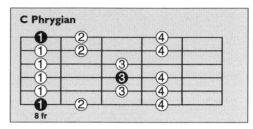

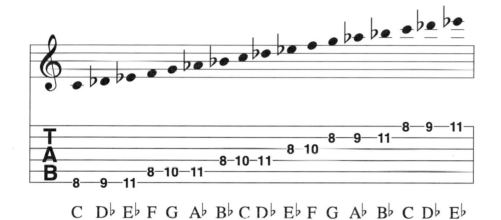

C D♭ E♭ F G A♭ B♭ C D♭ E♭ F G A♭ B♭ C D♭ E♭

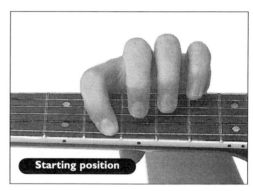

Spanish melody

This melody will give you a feel for the phrygian mode. Listen to the demonstration and then play along with the backing track.

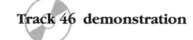 **Track 46 demonstration**    **Track 47 backing track**

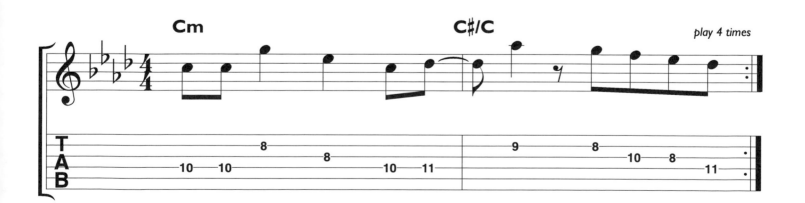

The lydian mode

C Lydian

This is a major type scale with a 'floating' feel, used by Steve Vai, Frank Zappa and John McLaughlin.

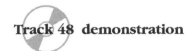 **Track 48 demonstration**

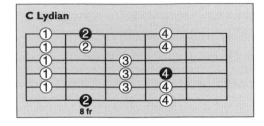

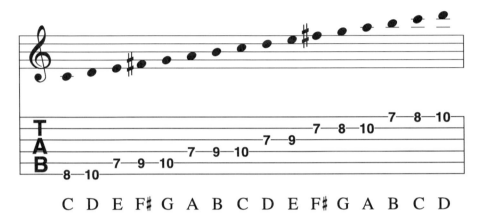

C D E F♯ G A B C D E F♯ G A B C D

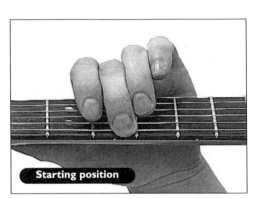

Starting position

Lydian riff

 **Track 49 demonstration**   **Track 50 backing track**

This riff highlights the character of the lydian mode.
Play it along with Track 50.

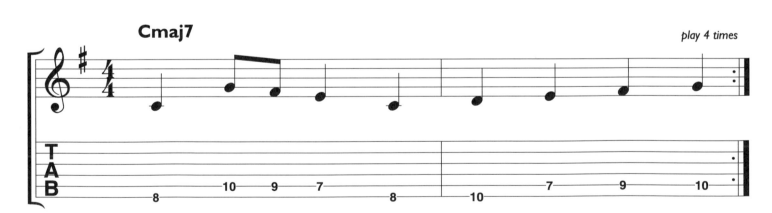

Cmaj7   *play 4 times*

C Mixolydian

This is a major type scale with a flattened seventh note, used by Eddie Van Halen and Crispian Mills.

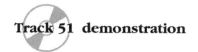 **Track 51 demonstration**

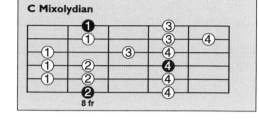

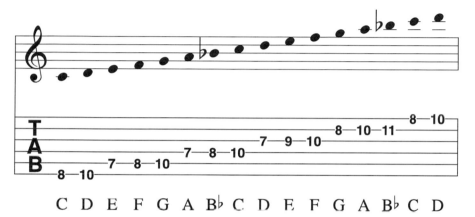

C D E F G A B♭ C D E F G A B♭ C D

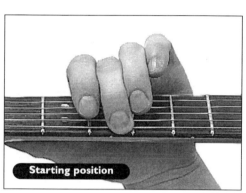

Starting position

Mixolydian exercise

Here's a little exercise using the mixolydian scale. It doesn't lend itself very well to riffs and solos!

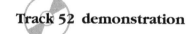 **Track 52 demonstration**   **Track 53 backing track**

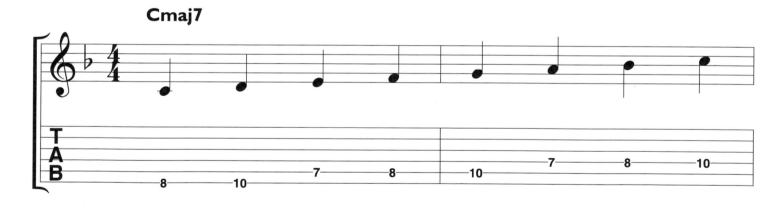

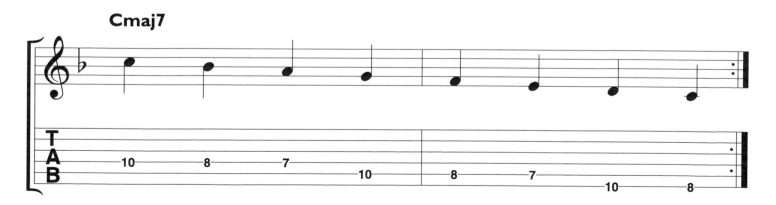

The locrian mode

C Locrian

This scale is unlike any of the other modes, and is not used much in popular music. See if you can create a solo using it!

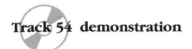

Track 54 demonstration

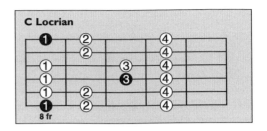

C Locrian

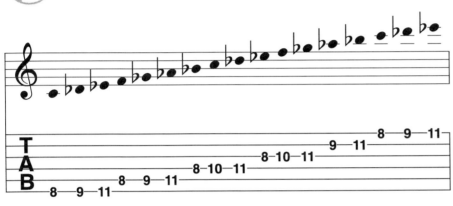

C Db Eb F Gb Ab Bb C Db Eb F Gb Ab Bb C Db Eb

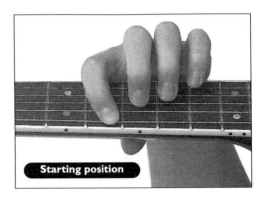

Starting position

There are many other types of scales but most of them are not commonly used in our 'Western' music system. Each different scale can be split up into its own family of modes so, as you can imagine, there's a mindboggling number out there!

However, you've learnt enough in this book to equip you for just about any type of solo or style of playing.

Playing up and down scales for hours is not only boring, but pointless. Make sure you regularly try out melodies or riffs while practising. On the right, you'll find some useful tips on soloing.

On the following page is a list of songs you may have heard of – or would like to play. With your new knowledge of scales, you'll find it much easier to play along and even work out how those famous solos were constructed. Good luck!

CONGRATULATIONS!

You can now:

- Play and use the seven modes – the building blocks of great guitar solos

- Play solos, riffs and licks using the major, minor, pentatonic, country and blues scales

- Read and understand tab, scale shapes and music notation

Soloing tips

- Try to phrase scale notes in a melodic way. Think of musical phrases that a singer might sing.

- Don't just play up and down a scale. It may work over the chord progression but it won't sound musical!

- Emphasise notes that work well with particular chords, such as the root and fifth of the scale.

- Don't play too many notes. Sometimes a few simple notes can say a lot more than a lot of hurried ones.

- Use techniques such as bends, hammer-ons and pull-offs to add interest to your solo.

Another Brick In The Wall (Pink Floyd)	D minor pentatonic, D dorian
Black Magic Woman (Santana)	D minor pentatonic, D aeolian
Bohemian Rhapsody (Queen)	C minor pentatonic, C aeolian
Don't Look Back In Anger (Oasis)	C major pentatonic
Easy Lover (Phil Collins)	F minor pentatonic, F aeolian
Johnny B. Goode (Chuck Berry)	B♭ mixolydian
Jump (Van Halen)	B♭ blues plus fast arpeggios
Hotel California (The Eagles)	B minor pentatonic, B aeolian
Legs (ZZ Top)	C♯ and F♯ minor pentatonic
Let It Be (The Beatles)	C major pentatonic
Little Wing (Jimi Hendrix)	E minor pentatonic, E aeolian, E phrygian
Livin' On A Prayer (Bon Jovi)	E aeolian
Out In The Fields (Gary Moore)	D aeolian
Purple Haze (Jimi Hendrix)	E dorian
Rosanna (Toto)	F mixolydian
Smoke On The Water (Deep Purple)	G minor pentatonic/aeolian, C dorian
Stairway To Heaven (Led Zeppelin)	A minor pentatonic
Sunday Bloody Sunday (U2)	B aeolian
Sunshine of Your Love (Eric Clapton)	D minor and major pentatonics
Time (Pink Floyd)	F♯ blues scale, F♯ aeolian
Too Much To Lose (Jeff Beck)	G blues, G mixolydian, G dorian
Wasted Years (Iron Maiden)	E aeolian, E minor pentatonic
Whole Lotta Love (Led Zeppelin)	E blues, E minor and major pentatonics

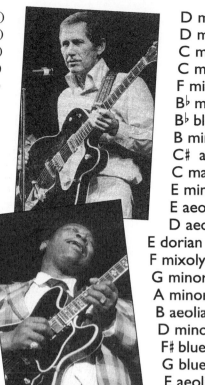

CD track list

Track 1	**Tuning Notes**	Track 28	**G major Shape 1**
Track 2	**Em pentatonic**	Track 29	**G major Shape 2**
Track 3	**E blues**	Track 30	**G major Shape 3**
Track 4	**Blues riff demo**	Track 31	**G major Shape 4**
Track 5	**Blues riff practice**	Track 32	**G major Shape 5**
Track 6	**Fm pentatonic**	Track 33	**Auld Lang Syne demo**
Track 7	**Gm pentatonic**	Track 34	**Auld Lang Syne practice**
Track 8	**12-bar blues riff demo**	Track 35	**G natural minor Shape 1**
Track 9	**12-bar blues riff practice**	Track 36	**G natural minor Shape 2**
Track 10	**Am pentatonic Shape 1**	Track 37	**G natural minor Shape 3**
Track 11	**Am pentatonic Shape 2**	Track 38	**G natural minor Shape 4**
Track 12	**Am pentatonic Shape 3**	Track 39	**G natural minor Shape 5**
Track 13	**Am pentatonic Shape 4**	Track 40	**Natural minor demo**
Track 14	**Am pentatonic Shape 5**	Track 41	**Natural minor practice**
Track 15	**Slide**	Track 42	**C Dorian**
Track 16	**Bend**	Track 43	**Dorian groove demo**
Track 17	**Bend & Release**	Track 44	**Dorian groove practice**
Track 18	**Lead guitar Lick 1**	Track 45	**C Phrygian**
Track 19	**Lead guitar Lick 2**	Track 46	**Spanish melody demo**
Track 20	**Lead guitar Lick 3**	Track 47	**Spanish melody practice**
Track 21	**Lead guitar Lick 4**	Track 48	**C Lydian**
Track 22	**12-bar blues solo in A demo**	Track 49	**Lydian riff demo**
Track 23	**12-bar blues solo in A practice**	Track 50	**Lydian riff practice**
Track 24	**A Major Pentatonic**	Track 51	**C Mixolydian**
Track 25	**A 'Country'**	Track 52	**Mixolydian exercise demo**
Track 26	**'Country' blues demo**	Track 53	**Mixolydian exercise practice**
Track 27	**'Country' blues practice**	Track 54	**C Locrian**

3/13 (186605)